The Rawlins Gallery is the home of a permanent exhibition, "The Genius of North Italian Stringed Instrument Making 1540-1793."

The Townsley Courtyard on a quiet winter evening.

The
SHRINE
TO MUSIC
MUSEUM

Photographed by Simon R. H. Spicer

Funds for publication of this book
provided in part
by the Beede Fund.

Produced by Companion Press
Santa Barbara, California

Jane Freeburg, Publisher

Edited by Mark Schlenz
Designed by Gay Hagen-Dunn

Printed in Korea
ISBN 0-944197-03-5
(hardcover) ISBN 0-944197-04-3
Library of Congress No: 87-063285

Cover: The rose of a guitar attributed
to Matteo Sellas, Venice, ca. 1640.
Ex. coll.: Bisiach. Witten-Rawlins
Collection, 1984.

Front Flap: Bass viola da gamba by
Johannes Florenus Guidantus, Bologna,
1728. Ex. coll.: Mackay-Smith.
Witten-Rawlins Collection, 1984.

Above: Harp, northern Italy,
ca. 1550. Ex. coll.: Bisiach.
Witten-Rawlins Collection, 1984.

Opposite: Tenor viola by Andrea
Guarneri, Cremona, 1664. This
famous tenor, like its counterpart, the
"Medici" tenor by Antonio Stradivari,
1690, now in Florence, and the violino
piccolo by the Brothers Amati, 1613,
in the Witten-Rawlins Collection
(see p. 10), is one of the three known
Cremonese instruments to have survived
in original condition. Ex. coll.: Bisiach.
Witten-Rawlins Collection, 1984.

Above: Detail of the "Harrison" violin by Antonio Stradivari, Cremona, 1693. A "long pattern" violin of the type made by Stradivari in the 1690s, it was chosen for illustration in color in the standard biography, Antonio Stradivari, *published in 1902 by W. E. Hill & Sons of London. Ex. coll.: Hottinger. Rawlins Fund, 1985.*

Opposite: Trombone by Michael Nagel, Nürnberg, 1656. Purchase funds given by Mr. and Mrs. Clifford E. Graese, Saddle River, New Jersey, 1985.

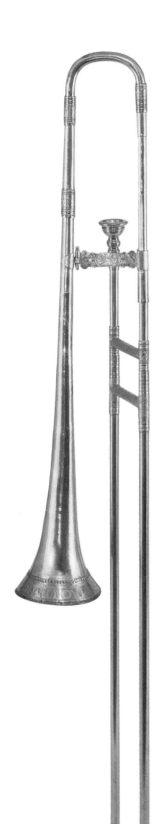

CONTENTS

Preface

The thousands of musical instruments preserved in the collections of The Shrine to Music Museum were all built and played by actual people living in real places at specific times. Unlike recent years, when musical instruments have often been viewed simply as utilitarian tools for the production of sound, most of the earlier instruments were also built to be admired for their craftsmanship and their visual beauty.

In the language of museums, musical instruments are three-dimensional objects, related to the other decorative arts; like early costumes, arms and armor, and 18th-century furniture, they are objects, happily, which combine both function and beauty of form. A trumpet from New Guinea, for instance, such as the superb example shown above, stands on its own as a work of so-called "primitive" art, quite aside from its function as a musical instrument. In Europe, Renaissance keyboard instruments sometimes carried the motto, "Pleasing to ear and eye alike."

Indeed, musical instruments were first collected as showpieces. The collection of Archduke Ferdinand of Tirol (d. 1596), once housed in the Schloss Ambras on a mountainside overlooking Innsbruck, but moved to the Kunsthistorisches Museum in Vienna by Kaiser Franz I in 1806, is the best-known example. Their role as works of decorative art is often the primary reason for the inclusion of musical instruments in art museums in this country and abroad such as The Metropolitan Museum of Art in New York, the Museum of Fine Arts in Boston, the Cincinnati Art Museum, and the Victoria

Left: Horn, Nepal, early 20th century. Inlaid coral and turquoise. Purchase funds given by Mrs. Clark Y. Gunderson, Vermillion, 1977. Drum, eastern Tibet, 19th century. Two human skull caps joined by a silver band. Ringley Fund, 1976.

Right: Taun trumpet, Mummeri village, Blackwater River, Middle Sepik, New Guinea, 19th century. Cowrie-shell eyes. Beede Fund, 1977.

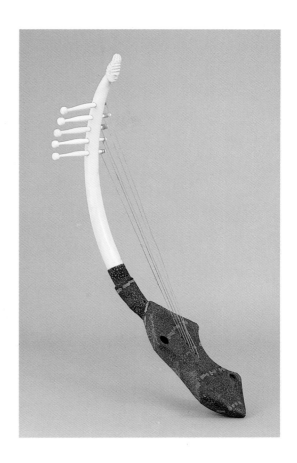

Left: Mayuri (peacock), northern India, 19th century. Ex. coll.: Allanson. Purchase funds given by Lydia and Edwin Downie, Hamilton, New York, 1981.

·Right: Arched harp, central Africa, 19th century. Ivory neck and pegs. Ex. coll.: Benkovic. Board of Trustees, 1978.

& Albert Museum in London among others. Curators at such institutions sometimes have difficulty justifying the acquisition of instruments that otherwise would fill gaps in their collections unless they are ornately decorated.

On the other hand, the social and cultural implications of musical instruments also make them important records of the civilizations of which they once were a part. Late-18th- and 19th-century instruments, in particular, clearly illustrate technological advancements growing out of the industrial revolution, as well as the role of music in society; hence, their presence in history and science/technology museums like the Deutsches Museum in Munich, the world's first great technical museum, the Henry Ford Museum in Dearborn, Michigan, and the many European museums devoted to a region's artistic, cultural, and/or social history, like the Germanisches Nationalmuseum in Nürnberg, the Museum Zeughaus in Innsbruck, the Gemeentemuseum in The Hague, and the Museum Carolino Augusteum in Salzburg.

Finally, because musical instruments, in the language of the anthropologist, are primary cultural indicators, large systematic collections, primarily of non-Western instruments, are often found in natural history museums, including the American Museum of Natural History in New York, the Field Museum in Chicago, and the Tropenmuseum in Amsterdam.

As an academic support unit of the University of South Dakota, the programs of The Shrine to Music Museum cut across all the

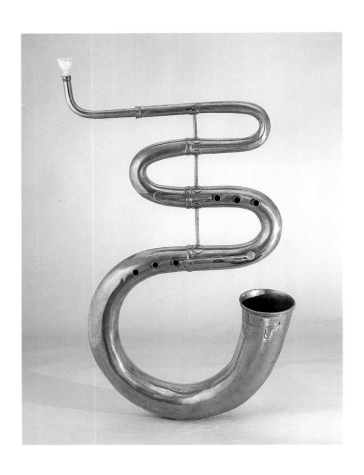

disciplines, and so do its collections. Most of the instruments in the Witten-Rawlins Collection, along with others from the Arne B. Larson Collection, as well as many of the more recent acquisitions, are showpieces equal to those found anywhere. They are remarkable works of exquisite craftsmanship and represent some of the finest achievements of our cultural heritage. On the other hand, the Museum's systematic collections, particularly of American and European wind instruments, will seldom, if ever, be shown in their entirety to the general public but are of great importance for comparative research. Only in this museum, for instance, can scholars find the vast resources needed to document the development of the great American manufacturers of brass, percussion, and woodwind instruments.

As America's only independent museum with a specific mission to serve as an international center for study of all aspects of the history of musical instruments, The Shrine to Music Museum, like the important musical instrument museums in Berlin, Leipzig, Munich, Paris, and other major European cities, is not subject to the constraints that sometimes hamper the development of important instrument collections that are part of

Left: Strohviol, London, early 20th century. Used for early recordings, later as a novelty in vaudeville shows. Arne B. Larson Collection, 1979.

Right: English guitar by J.N. Preston, London, after 1734. Watch-key tuning. Fitted with Smith's Patent Box by which small hammers strike the strings. Original case. Arne B. Larson Collection, 1979.

larger, more diverse institutions. Perhaps it is that freedom to develop that has been most responsible for the remarkable achievements that are now a source of great pride for the donors, patrons, staff, trustees, volunteers, and others who shared the adventure and helped make the dream come true.

The goal of the Board of Trustees, simply put, has been to build the finest collections of their kind in the world. The ultimate degree to which that goal can be achieved does not really matter. Just as it is foolish to argue which art collections are the greatest — those at the British Museum, the Hermitage, the Louvre, The Metropolitan Museum of Art, the Uffizi Gallery, or wherever (the point being that each is great in its own way) — so, too, is it foolish to argue the relative merits of musical instrument collections. European holdings tend to be regional in scope, rather than comprehensive, but have great depth in certain areas. The Shrine to Music Museum may not always be able to match that depth, but many times it can — and its holdings are much broader in scope.

Whatever the measure, the Museum's collections, as they have now developed, are among the greatest in the world, and it is essential that they be preserved properly. Ultimately, it is a museum's collections that make it great, but with great collections come awesome responsibilities for their preservation. That is the challenge for the future.

André P. Larson
Director

The Shrine to Music Museum

Located on a bluff overlooking the Missouri River basin near where the Lewis & Clark expedition camped in 1804, Vermillion, South Dakota, is a small, typical Midwestern college town of 10,000 people. Not so typical is The Shrine to Music Museum, housed on the campus of the University of South Dakota, which is the home of some of the most important collections of rare, antique musical instruments to be found in the Western Hemisphere.

Founded in 1973 by the South Dakota Regents of Education, The Shrine to Music Museum & Center for Study of the History of Musical Instruments is one of the great institutions of its kind in the world. Its ever-growing collections, which include more than 4,500 musical instruments from virtually all of the world's cultures and historical periods, are among the most comprehensive anywhere. The Museum's rise to world-class status has been little short of meteoric, and its holdings now rank in size and importance with those of the great instrument collections in Berlin, Brussels, Munich, Paris, and Vienna.

The Arne B. Larson Collection of Musical Instruments & Library, the largest collection still in private hands when it was donated to the Museum in 1979, is the nucleus of the Museum's holdings. Unlike other such collections, which specialize in only one or two of three broad areas — American, European, and non-Western instruments — the Larson Collection has substantial holdings in all three areas, with particular strength in American and European winds. It contains more than 2,500 instruments, plus an extensive supporting library of books, music, periodicals, photographs, sound recordings, and related musi-

cal memorabilia. The National Association of Schools of Music calls it, "Certainly one of the greatest collections of musical instruments in the world."

In 1982-83 the Museum's holdings were further enriched by the gift of a collection of 145 woodwinds assembled by Wayne Sorensen of Los Gatos, California. In addition to important 19th-century flutes, clarinets, and oboes — Sorensen's collecting specialty was "early Boehm-system clarinets and flutes and early key systems" — there were also boxes of documentary materials, including books, catalogs, music, and photographs.

Then, on February 5, 1984, the Museum purchased the Witten Family Collection of early Italian stringed instruments, bows, tools, labels, and documentary source materials, including 16th-century books and prints. Long recognized as the greatest collection of its kind in the Western Hemisphere and one of the top two or three collections of stringed instruments in the world, it consists of seventy-five violins, violas, 'cellos, viols, lutes, guitars, and other instruments by the great 16th-, 17th-, and 18th-century masters, including three generations of the Amati family, Magnus Tieffenbrucker, Gasparo da Salò, Matteo Sellas, Andrea Guarneri, and others, plus twenty-five important bows. Included are three of the fourteen known surviving instruments by Andrea Amati (d. 1577), the 16th-century Cremonese craftsman in whose shop the form of the instruments of the violin family as we know them today crystallized.

14 Acquisition of the Witten-Rawlins Collection, as it is now known,

Left: This nine-foot-tall slit drum from Ambrym Island in the South Pacific crossed the ocean on the Columbus Line freighter "Virginia" in 1981, and now stands guard at the entrance to the Beede Gallery (see p. 26).

Right: The Museum often loans instruments for major exhibitions at other institutions; in 1982-83 this "rain-catcher" Sousaphone was shown at the New York Historical Society, the Dallas Historical Society, the New York State Museum in Albany, and the Milwaukee Public Museum.

Below: Drums, Uganda, early 20th century. Collected by Carl E. Akeley (1864-1926), American explorer and naturalist. Gift of Melville H. Miller, DeLand, Florida, 1983.

ended an international struggle to acquire it, keeping a remarkable assemblage of early instruments in the United States and catapulting The Shrine to Music Museum onto the international stage. Writing in the *New York Sunday Times*, the music critic Tim Page noted that the purchase "is believed to represent the largest sum ever paid by a museum for a collection of antique musical instruments."

Finally, additional instruments continue to be received as gifts and bequests, through exchange with other museums, and by purchase on the international market with private funding by the Museum's Board of Trustees.

The Board initiated its aggressive acquisitions program in 1975 to provide the resources needed to accomplish the Museum's stated mission: 1) to assemble and to preserve systematic collections of musical instruments, encyclopedic in scope, representative of all of the world's cultures and historical periods; 2) to assemble and to preserve a major supporting library of music, books, periodicals, photographs, sound recordings, and musical memorabilia; and 3) to serve as an international center for study of the history of musical instruments, providing resources for cultural, humanistic,

and musical scholarship.

Since then, hundreds of instruments have been acquired, most of them as gifts and others by purchase on the international market. The Trustees consider the acquisition program to be their primary responsibility, and they support the effort magnificently.

Although the Museum must always be ready to take advantage of opportunities as they present themselves, a special effort has been made to fill identified gaps and weaknesses in the Museum's collections in systematic fashion. First priority was given to non-Western instruments. The goal was to round out the collections with instruments of high quality so that the Museum would have representative examples from the various non-Western societies. That task was well met by 1979. A second, on-going project is the increasingly-selective acquisition of those American instruments needed to strengthen the Museum's already-preeminent holdings in that area. A third, on-going priority has been the selective enhancement of the Museum's European wind instruments, including a myriad of rare 16th-, 17th-, and 18th-century examples, many made of ivory, by the master craftsmen of Dresden, Nürnberg, Paris, and other important early centers of musical instrument making.

Space constraints, at least for the moment, preclude a move to develop an encyclopedic collection of keyboard instruments, but the Museum is committed to the development of a highly-selective collection of representative examples, and has made great strides in that regard, including English, Flemish, French, and Italian harpsichords; German clavichords; a tangentenflügel by Späth & Schmahl, Regens-

Above: Bob Rawlins, Balboa Island, California (left) watches Marge Rawlins cut the ribbon to open the Rawlins Gallery on May 8, 1986, as Mr. and Mrs. Laurence C. Witten II, Fairfield, Connecticut (right) look on. Others watching (from the left) are Arne B. Larson, who in 1979 donated the vast collection which is the nucleus of the Museum's holdings, and Genevieve Truran, Professor Emerita of Music at USD, with whom Mrs. Rawlins studied piano as an undergraduate. The gallery houses much of the Witten-Rawlins Collection acquired in 1984, plus important stringed instruments purchased since then with the Rawlins Fund and the Arne B. and Jeanne F. Larson Endowment Fund.

"A museum's collections make it great, but with great collections come awesome responsibilities."

Left: The Rawlins Gallery documents the history of Italian violin-making with priceless examples that survive in as nearly original condition as can be found.

Right: Usher Abell of Vermillion, a founding Trustee, plays the "Harrison," the great violin by Antonio Stradivari acquired by the Museum (Rawlins Fund) in 1985. Watching (left to right) are Barnes Abell, then President of the Board of Trustees (1973-1986); Martin P. Busch, the Board's first President (1972-73); and Geoffrey Fushi of Bein & Fushi, Inc. in Chicago, who says the "Harrison" is "probably the grandest concert violin made before the year 1700."

burg, 1784; and a number of early English and Viennese pianos.

The major endeavor during the early '80s, however, was to acquire important European stringed instruments. Purchase of the Witten-Rawlins Collection, along with other selective acquisitions, including the "Harrison" violin of 1693 and the "Rawlins" guitar of 1700, both by Antonio Stradivari, soon filled that last remaining gap in spectacular fashion.

Today, although acquisitions have become increasingly selective, about 100 instruments are still received each year, continuing the Museum's policy of filling specific needs with the finest examples available. Values can range anywhere from a few thousand dollars to half a million or more. Still, placing a dollar figure on the Museum's holdings would be difficult — and probably futile. Declining to confirm the current market value of the Museum's holdings (in the millions of dollars), the Trustees note that the Museum's collections contain many instruments that are among the earliest, best preserved, and historically most important examples that survive, and such collections can never again be duplicated. In cultural and historical terms, they are priceless.

The Museum's collections are used extensively for scholarly research. Students and faculty from the University of South Dakota, students and faculty from many other major American colleges and universities, and scholars from abroad all make frequent use of the Museum's specialized resources — its staff, its library, and its collections. The University of South Dakota offers the M.M. degree with a concentration in the history of musical instruments, the only accredited pro-

gram of its kind offered by an American institution of higher learning, and theses and doctoral dissertations based on the Museum's holdings have been written not only at USD, but also at such diverse institutions as the University of Oklahoma, Louisiana State University, Michigan State University, West Virginia University, and others.

The Museum's public galleries are designed to help visitors discover the wonder of musical instruments as examples of inventive workmanship, as objects of refined beauty, and as artifacts representative of the central position which music has played in all of the world's cultures and historical periods.

Other facilities include the Arne B. Larson Concert Hall, where superb acoustics and an intimate atmosphere provide a perfect setting for the performance of music played on original instruments of various historical periods and cultural milieu. A tea room, a library, extensive study-storage areas, and a laboratory for the conservation and restoration of the instruments are also part of the Museum.

The building, originally built as a Carnegie library in 1910, is a three-story, 20,000-square-foot structure faced with Indiana limestone. Its interior decoration, splendidly restored to its original condition, features an interplay of dark oak, marble wainscotting, and terrazzo floors. The year-long, $1-million restoration project, completed in early 1986, also provided a sophisticated climate-control system that maintains the critical humidity and temperature levels needed to preserve the instruments. The building is fully accessible to the handicapped.

Dedication ceremonies to mark the completion of the renovation

Left: The Baltimore Consort is one of the many important ensembles that have played amid the special ambience and superb acoustics of the Arne B. Larson Concert Hall since it opened in 1986. Others include the Amsterdam Loeki Stardust Quartet, The Folger Consort, London Baroque, the Classical Quartet, Music from Aston Magna, the Lieberman-Kroll Duo, the Smithson String Quartet, and many more.

Right: A candlelit concert in the Beede Gallery features the music of Schubert played on the Museum's lyraflügel (upright piano) by Johann Christian Schleip, Berlin, ca. 1825. Rawlins Fund, 1982.

Above: The Abell Family Gallery exhibits many of the Museum's magnificent keyboard instruments—ornately-decorated English, Flemish, French, and Italian harpsichords of the 17th and 18th centuries, German clavichords, and a wide variety of early pianos.

Below: Lovingly restored in 1985-86, the Museum's interior features an interplay of dark oak, fanciful plaster work, terrazzo floors, and marble wainscotting.

and the opening of new galleries were held May 8-11, 1986, and included an international conference, sponsored by the American Musical Instrument Society and the Midwest chapter of the American Musicological Society, that attracted guests from Canada, England, Italy, Poland, and West Germany, as well as from across the United States. Dedicatory recitals in the Arne B. Larson Concert Hall were played by Richard Luby, Baroque violin, and Arthur Haas, harpsichord, the Boland-Dowdall Duo, and Paul O'Dette, lute.

A year later, the Townsley Courtyard, complete with a fountain and four bronze sculptures, was built in front of the Museum. It was dedicated September 26, 1987, and has become a natural extension of the ambience that makes the museum itself such a special place.

19

The Townsley Courtyard

Visitors to The Shrine to Music Museum enter through the Townsley Courtyard, a lovely oasis where they are welcomed by four bronze figures: a turn-of-the-century immigrant violinist and three children. The grace and charm of the sculpture are accompanied by the peaceful music of a fountain's cascading water. Prominent Black Hills sculptor Michael R. Tuma was commissioned by the Museum's Board of Trustees to create the statues, representing the Dakota musical heritage in celebration of the South Dakota Centennial.

With walls of Indiana limestone cut to match the patterns found in the Museum's facade, the courtyard was designed by the architect Donald R. Baltzer to look as if it could have been part of the original building, constructed in 1910. The fountain is 22 feet in diameter with two tiers of falling water. A large Norway emerald queen maple, imperial locusts, and conifers shade the area. There are benches for restful reflection and a miniature amphitheatre for outdoor performances.

The Townsley Courtyard was a gift to the Vermillion community from Mr. and Mrs. R. E. Rawlins of Balboa Island, California, in memory of Mrs. Rawlins' parents, John Boyd Townsley — who graduated from the University of South Dakota in 1900 — and his wife, Emeline C. Townsley. The courtyard is just one of many important contributions that Mr. and Mrs. Rawlins have made to the museum and the cultural life of their native state.

Left: The Symphony Brass played fanfares during the dedication of the Townsley Courtyard and the unveiling of a fountain featuring four bronze figures by the Black Hills sculptor Michael R. Tuma.

Above: More than 1,000 balloons were released to help celebrate the occasion.

Above: Bob Rawlins (left) of Balboa Island, California, Michael R. Tuma, sculptor, and John A. Day, Dean of the USD College of Fine Arts, visited together after the dedication ceremonies.

Top right: Four bronze figures atop the fountain represent an immigrant violinist and three children.

Center right: Mr. and Mrs. R. E. Rawlins were honored on the occasion for having brought international recognition to the University through their gifts to the Museum and the College of Fine Arts. Governor George Mickelson declared September 26 "Bob and Marge Rawlins Day" in South Dakota.

Below: Young and old alike enjoyed the fountain's cascading water.

21

The Arne B. Larson Collection

Left: Casper and Oliane Larson sit in front of their southern Minnesota farm home about 1895. Their son Adolph stands behind them holding his violin. His son Arne B. Larson would be born in the house in 1904. Later, the house burned to the ground, a tragedy indelibly marked in the memory of Arne B., who was then 12 years old.

Right: Arne B. plays a Swedish nyckleharpa (see p. 53) in the living room of his home in Brookings in the late 1950s.

Arne B. Larson was born in 1904 in a southern Minnesota farmhouse built by his grandparents a few miles from the small town of Hanska. One of nine musically-inclined sons and daughters of Adolf and Barbara Larson, he began playing instruments at age six and was soon performing Sundays with the family orchestra at the Nora Church, a Unitarian enclave which still stands "on the hill" near Hanska. Later he organized the Searles Silver Cornet Band to provide entertainment for area residents. In the 1920s he began collecting instruments made obsolete by Congressional legislation lowering the pitch standard for A to 440 vibrations per second.

Initially, Arne's choice of careers was a source of contention between him and his father. The elder Larson was a fine musician, but believed that those who tried to make their living that way ended up playing in taverns "and all that lowdown stuff." In any case, as the oldest son, Arne was simply *expected* to take over the family farm. However, disagreements about old and new agricultural practices — Arne wanted to try hybrid seeds and other "newfangled things" — furthered the rift between father and son. During the Depression of the '30s, Arne set off, literally with a nickel in his pocket and cardboard in his shoes, for the Minneapolis College of Music.

Earning a degree there (later he also earned an M.M. degree at Northwestern University in Evanston, Illinois), Arne landed a teaching job in Little Falls, Minnesota, where his bands and orchestras won state championships. Later he moved to International Falls; then, in January 1943, Arne brought his young wife, family, and collection of

Left: Arne B. Larson works at his desk in the "teaching collection," where for years he demonstrated a variety of unique instruments for thousands of Museum visitors.

Right: Lieutenant Governor Lowell C. Hansen II (left) and Arne B. and Jeanne F. Larson cut the ribbon to open a new gallery in 1981. Looking on (left to right) are Charles D. Lein, USD President (1977-82); William J. Srstka, Jr., President of the Board of Regents; and Wayne S. Knutson, USD Vice-President.

instruments to South Dakota and accepted a job as Head of the Music Department in the Brookings Public Schools.

Meanwhile, old instruments were a continuing passion for him. "I would read about old instruments and always wanted to know what they sounded like," he explains. During the years surrounding World War II, he found that many people in devastated European countries were eager to exchange instruments for tea and canned goods. Unable to travel to Europe on a teacher's salary, Arne made contacts any way he could through journals and by letter. In fact, his modest teacher's salary was always turned over to his wife, Jeanne, to sustain the family. Arne earned everything he spent on what was then his "hobby" by tuning pianos on weekends — often traveling to neighboring towns by train.

Gradually he developed a network of contacts to help him locate obscure instruments. Missionaries traveling in Africa, India, and the Orient brought back unusual pieces. In the early 1950s Arne wrote to world traveler and commentator Lowell Thomas, who was preparing for a journey to Tibet, and asked him to watch for exotic instruments. He had all but forgotten about the letter when a carefully-boxed instrument — a unique, serpentine Tibetan horn — arrived months later from the famed journalist.

Eventually the collection amassed in the Larson home numbered more than 2,000 instruments. "Of course the neighbors thought he was nuts," say Arne's children of their father's obsession. "It was a big house, but there were rooms you couldn't walk into because of all the instruments — you would open a door and stuff was piled to the ceiling."

23

Arne B., as everyone in Brookings called him, rarely paid more than a couple of dollars for an instrument, but he loved each of them — repairing those in need and learning to play each as he got them, even the most esoteric. As the collection grew, he also developed a public program during which he would demonstrate 50 or so of the instruments for church, school, and civic groups.

Meanwhile, Arne's reputation as a band and orchestra conductor grew. Brookings consistently brought home top awards from musical competitions. In 1962 the community sent Arne B. and his students to the Seattle World's Fair. By 1964 most of the Larson children were grown and the house was nearly filled to capacity with valuable musical instruments. Ready for a career change that would involve his overwhelming hobby, Arne began looking for institutions interested in his collection. Several colleges and universities in urban centers distant from South Dakota responded, but Arne had no desire to leave the Midwest.

I. D. Weeks, President of the University of South Dakota (1935-66), expressed interest in the collection and invited Arne to come to Vermillion as Professor of Music. Usher Abell, Chairman of the Department of Music, joined Weeks and Warren M. "Doc" Lee, Dean of the College of Fine Arts, in lobbying for Arne's move to Vermillion. In 1966 he accepted the position, and that summer a number of fully-loaded grain trucks rolled down the highway, each carrying hundreds of instruments from the Larson home in Brookings to the University in Vermillion.

On April 6, 1979, Arne and his wife, Jeanne, officially donated the

Top: As important as collecting was to him, conducting was the overwhelming passion in Arne B. Larson's life. Here, at age 78, he conducts the Dalesburg Community Band for the 113th-annual Midsummer Festival at the Dalesburg Lutheran Church, 13 miles north of Vermillion, in 1982.

Right: The Shrine to Music Museum was recognized as "A Landmark of American Music" by the National Music Council in 1976.

*Left: In 1973 Arne traveled to Pitts-
burgh, Pennsylvania, to do two programs with Fred Rogers, creator and
host of Mister Rogers' Neighborhood,
the longest-running children's televison
show on the PBS network. An estimated
audience of more than four million
saw the programs, which have since
been rerun on numerous occasions.*

*Right: School children from the four-
state area tour the Museum on a regular
basis. In 1984 Arne demonstrated
this Scandinavian lur for 3rd graders
from Vermillion.*

collection — which, by then, numbered more than 2,500 instruments
and was valued at more than $1 million — to the State of South Dakota.
Governor William Janklow presided over an impressive ceremony held
to honor them for their extraordinary generosity.

They were honored again in 1983, when the Museum's Board of
Trustees established the Arne B. & Jeanne F. Larson Endowment Fund
with $332,000 from the sale of the 160-acre Minnesota farm (where
Arne was born), which had been owned by the Larson family for more
than 100 years. The principal was invested and will remain intact; use
of the resultant investment earnings is specifically restricted to "the
purchase of additional acquisitions designed to strengthen the holdings
of The Shrine to Music Museum."

Arne, a natural entertainer, has delighted countless Museum visitors by performing tunes on various instruments, telling stories, and
giving tours. For years his has been the personality of the place. Being
a great collector is not always the same, however, as being a museum
person. His collection developed as an extension of his ego. It was a
private part of him...and all of a sudden it was institutionalized and
there were other people working with it and cataloging it. There were
stresses and strains.

Now, however, the most important thing to Arne is that his collection is receiving wonderful care, yet has remained in his native Midwest.
When questioned about the Museum's location, he answers, with a
twinkle in his eye, "It's no farther from New York to Vermillion than it
is from Vermillion to New York."

25

Left: A nine-foot-tall slit drum from Ambrym Island in the South Pacific stands like a sentinel just inside the entrance to the Grace L. Beede Gallery, where many of the Museum's most exotic instruments are exhibited.

Above: The people of Ambrym Island raise pigs, the principal source of wealth with which to purchase a higher rank in society. As James Michener writes in Tales of the South Pacific, the most valuable pigs are those whose tusks grow in a complete circle until they penetrate the animal's jaw. The pig is then sacrificed, a feast is held, and the vertical slit drums, carved in secrecy, are erected and played for dancing. Board of Trustees, 1981.

NON-WESTERN
INSTRUMENTS

Here is the enigma, the romance, the mystery of the unknown...instruments from the great civilizations of Africa, Asia, and the South Pacific...a zither built as a crocodile...a magnificent Burmese harp...an Indian mayuri, shaped like a peacock...hand-painted Persian instruments...exotic, hand-carved drums from the jungles of New Guinea...all of them evocative of adventure in distant lands.

Top: Taun trumpet, Mummeri village, Blackwater River, Middle Sepik, New Guinea, 19th century. Beede Fund, 1977.

Right: Drum, Batak tribe, Sumatra (Indonesia), 19th century. Bottom carved to resemble old bronze cannon; traces of green pigment remain. Board of Trustees, 1977. Handle drum, probably from Samoa, early 20th century. Arne B. Larson Collection, 1979. Handle drum, Trobriand Islands, early 20th century. Board of Trustees, 1976.

Below: Mamboo flute (detail), Mirenbei village, Middle Sepik, New Guinea, early 20th century. The head is a stylized rhinobird. Board of Trustees, 1977.

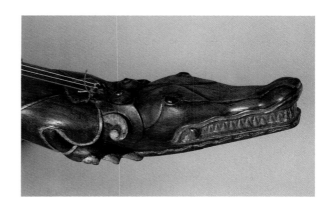

*" . . . all of them evocative of
adventure in distant lands."*

*Top left: Saùng-gauk, Burma, 19th/20th
century. A highly-decorated arched
harp, originally associated with Buddhist
royal dynasties, now the national instrument of Burma. Beede Fund, 1978.*

*Top right: Mi gyaun, Mon people,
Burma, 19th century. A crocodile-
shaped zither with ivory-tipped tuning
pegs at the tail-end carved in the shape
of lotus bulbs. Beede Fund, 1979.*

*Left: Tro, Mon people, Burma, 19th
century. This spike fiddle is an amalgam
of Eastern and Western influences. Ex.
coll.: de Bricqueville. Purchase funds
given by LeRoy G. Hoffman, Eureka,
South Dakota, 1980.*

Bottom right: Mayuri, northern India, 19th century. This peacock is a bowed stringed instrument with movable frets, four principal strings, and fifteen sympathetic strings. Ex. coll.: Allanson. Purchase funds given by Lydia and Edwin Downie, Hamilton, New York, 1981.

Center right: Restoration of the hand-painted peacock required many hours of delicate, tedious inpainting to return the instrument to its former splendor.

Far right: Máhorá thérk (detail), Siam (Thailand), ca. 1630-80. A procession of animals associated with the rainy season—elephants, snails, and a lizard— make their way across the incurved side of this cast-bronze drum, which is used to invoke the spirits of the clouds. Rawlins Fund, 1980.

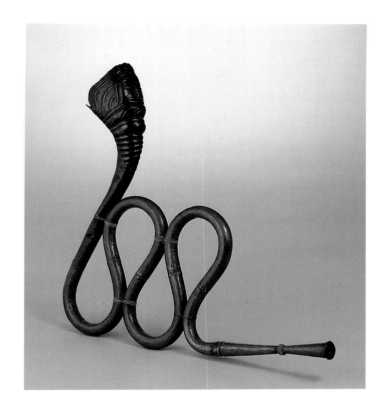

Top left: Shakuhachi, Japan, 19th century. Arne B. Larson Collection, 1979. Chikuzen-biwa (short-necked lute), Japan, early 20th century. Board of Trustees, 1976.

Left: Wood block and slit drum, China, early 20th century. Arne B. Larson Collection, 1979.

Above: Nagphani, Tibet, 20th century. A serpentine horn with a face in repoussé on the bell. Given to Arne B. Larson by the famous newscaster Lowell Thomas. Arne B. Larson Collection, 1979.

Below left: Dung-dkar, Reting Monastery area, Lhasa, Tibet, 19th century. A pair of conch-shell horns used in Buddhist ritual music. Ringley Fund, 1976.

Top: Hand-painted, 19th-century Persian instruments highlight an exhibit of instruments from Western Asia. Purchase funds given by Barnes and Usher Abell, Vermillion, 1978.

Top right: The delicate rose of this 19th-century 'ud is reminiscent of Moorish architecture. Arne B. Larson Collection, 1979.

Right: Kalengo, Nigeria, early 20th century. The pitch of this drum is changed by squeezing the cords and altering the tension of the heads. Arne B. Larson Collection, 1979.

Below: Drum (detail), Uganda, early 20th century. Inside a fetish rattles around; what it is will remain a mystery as long as the drum stays intact. Gift of Melville H. Miller, DeLand, Florida, 1983.

EUROPEAN BRASS & PERCUSSION

The glitter and the sparkle of European court life... the spectacle of the parade ground... finely-crafted horns, trumpets, and trombones by the great artisans of 17th- and 18th-century Nürnberg... "serpents" made of wood covered with leather, but "brass" instruments nevertheless... the technological developments of the industrial revolution... all reflect the ageless, universal power of human ingenuity and imagination.

Left: Many of the Museum's important brass instruments are exhibited in the Mr. and Mrs. Hubert H. Everist Gallery.

Top right: Trombones have been associated with the underworld from Monteverdi's Orfeo to Mozart's Don Giovanni and snakes are a favorite decorative motif, as seen on this trombone by C.G. Schuster, Markneukirchen, Germany, ca. 1890. Arne B. Larson Collection, 1979.

Above: Trombone (detail), France, 19th century. Dragon-head bells were popular in European military bands of the early 19th century. Arne B. Larson Collection, 1979.

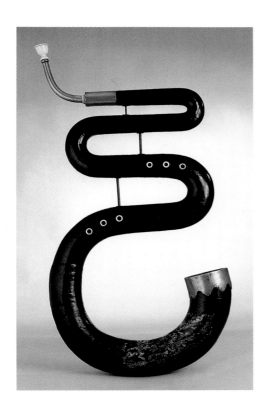

Above: Serpent, England, early 19th century. The coat of arms includes a lion and a mounted charger on either side of a crest, bordered on the bottom by a blue ribbon with the words [MEL]TO[N] BAND. Arne B. Larson Collection, 1979.

Top right: Keyed bugle by Thomas Key, 20 Charing Cross, London, ca. 1813. Board of Trustees, 1978. Keyed bugle by Charles Pace, 40 King Street, London, ca. 1834-49. Arne B. Larson Collection, 1979. Keyed bugle with oyster-shell keys, probably England, ca. 1825. Arne B. Larson Collection, 1979.

Right: Flügelhorn with case by Henry Distin, London, ca. 1856. Ringley Fund, 1975.

Far right: Bugle by August Heinrich Rott, Prague, ca. 1850. Board of Trustees, 1984.

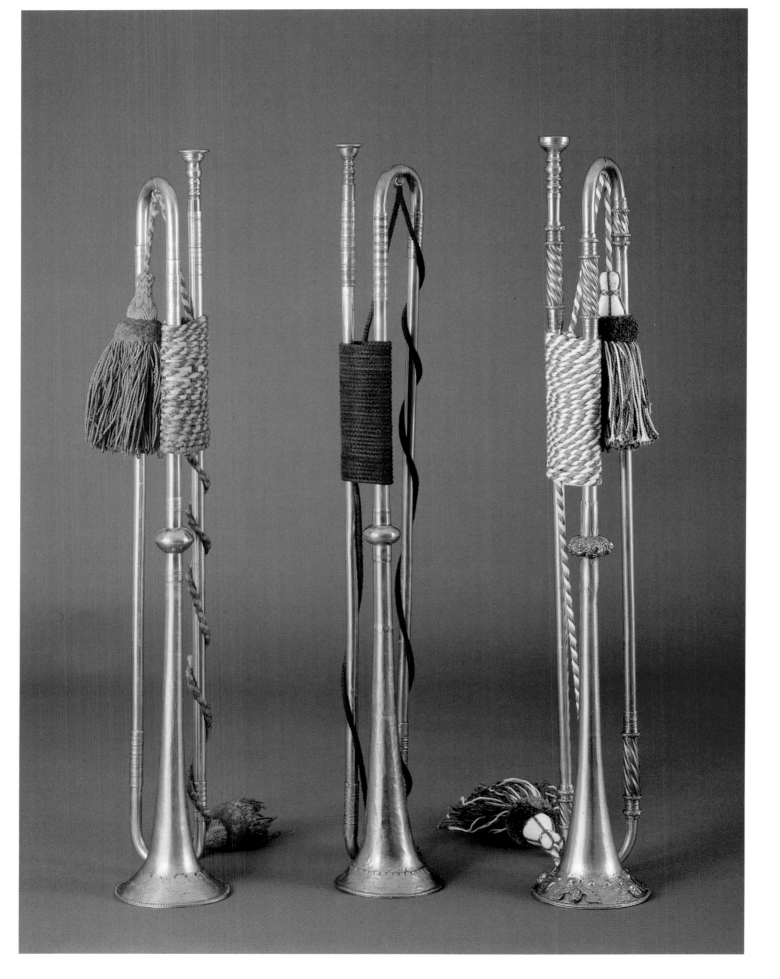

". . . reflect the ageless, universal power of human ingenuity and imagination."

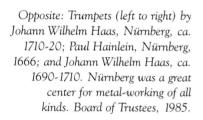

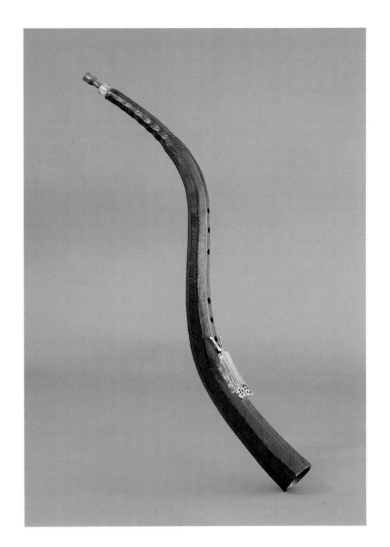

Opposite: Trumpets (left to right) by Johann Wilhelm Haas, Nürnberg, ca. 1710-20; Paul Hainlein, Nürnberg, 1666; and Johann Wilhelm Haas, ca. 1690-1710. Nürnberg was a great center for metal-working of all kinds. Board of Trustees, 1985.

Above: Detail of the bell of the trumpet by J.W. Haas, ca. 1690-1710, showing the rabbit (Hase is the German word for hare) which is the family symbol. The rabbit looks back over his shoulder on instruments made by the son and the grandson.

Right: Tenor zink (cornetto), Germany, mid-17th century. Ex. coll.: Canon Galpin. Board of Trustees, 1984.

Below: Tromba da caccia (coiled trumpet) by Friedrich Steinmez, Nürnberg, after 1694. Two other examples survive in Berlin. Gift of Barbara and Burton E. Hardin, Charleston, Illinois, 1986.

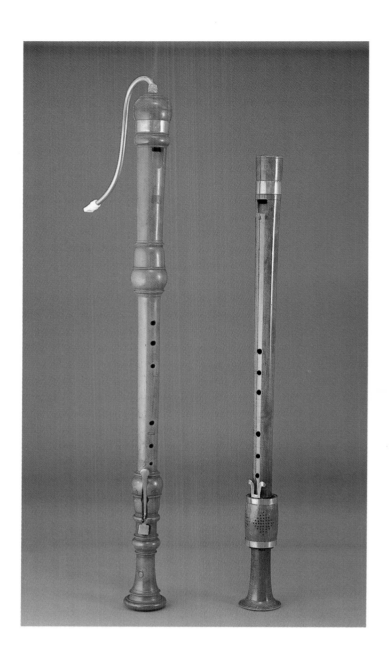

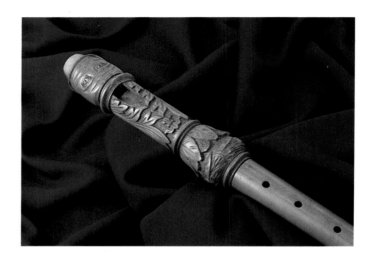

EUROPEAN WOODWINDS

Flutes made of ivory with a single key of gold or silver... a Renaissance recorder played at Bohemia's Rožmberk court... the graceful, slender profile of an ivory oboe... Baroque recorders, ornately carved... basset horns, Mozart, and Masonic symbolism... the intricate key systems of the 19th century... superb instruments built to play the haunting melodies of the great composers of Western civilization.

Left: Bass recorder in F (left) by Johann Christoph Denner, Nürnberg, late 17th century. Ex. coll.: de Bricqueville. Board of Trustees, 1985. Bass (basset) recorder in G by the Rožmberk master, Bohemia, ca. 1552-99. Branded twice just below the windway exit is the stamp of a yet-unidentified maker whose stamp is also found on five instruments inventoried at the Hofkappelle in Rožmberk, near Prachatitz, Bohemia, in 1599 and 1610. The Rožmberk court band, organized in 1552 and enlarged during the following half-century, owned 175 instruments, twelve of which survive today in the Národní Muzeum in Prague. Ex. coll.: Canon Galpin. Arne B. and Jeanne F. Larson Endowment Fund, 1985.

Above: Treble (alto) recorder by Johann Benedikt Gahn, Nürnberg, before 1711. Boxwood, ornately carved. Rawlins Fund, 1987.

"... built to play the haunting melodies of the great composers of Western civilization."

Above: Oboe d'amore by Johann Wolfgang Kenigsperger, Roding (?), before 1752. Three keys. Arne B. and Jeanne F. Larson Endowment Fund, 1986.

Right: Flute by Martin, Potsdam, Germany, 1822. Two additional upper joints for pitch changes. Arne B. Larson Collection, 1979. Clarinet in B-flat by Goulding & Company, London, before 1836. Arne B. Larson Collection, 1979. Clarinet in high G by F. Czermak, Prague, ca. 1810. Board of Trustees, 1985.

Details, below: Clarinet bell by Caroli, Clusone, Italy, ca. 1795. Boxwood, ornately carved. Gift of Bernhard von Hünerbein, Cologne, West Germany, 1987.

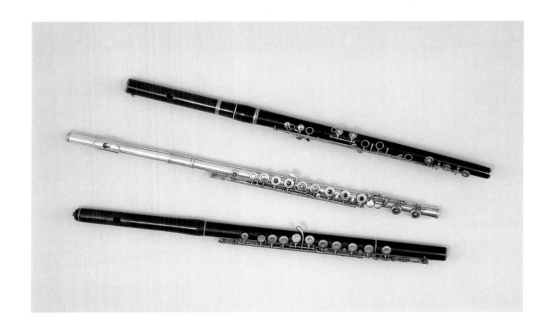

The Wayne Sorensen Collection

Top: Flutes (top to bottom) by Cornelius Ward, London, with the key system patented by Ward in 1842; Louis Lot, Paris, ca. 1855-75; and Boehm & Mendler, Munich, after 1867. Wayne Sorensen Collection, 1982-83.

Above. W. Wayne Sorensen.

Willard Wayne Sorensen was born July 10, 1918, in Pocatello, Idaho, a reputed "band town" with interest in all forms of musical entertainment. The Philharmonic Band and Orchestra Society was the oldest musical organization in the city, with offices in the opera house block as early as 1894.

The Gate City Silver Band was the forerunner of the many bands for which Pocatello was famous. It won laurels all over the state and in 1896 was recognized as the state's "crack band." In 1904 the Eagle Band was organized and attired in dazzling uniforms. The Citizen's Band was formed in 1906.

Shortly after World War I, the Italian Band was established. The musicians came from Naples, Italy, to work in the railroad shops. Many of them were graduates of the Naples Conservatory. The band became the Oregon Short Line shop employees' band, with 50 musicians, and had a great influence on Sorensen's life. In 1928 it became the official city band and remained so until 1931, at which time both the city and the Union Pacific railroad withdrew their support.

In the meantime, the Pocatello High School Band had been organized. In 1932 Sorensen joined the group as oboist. His family had little money, and the only instrument available was an oboe. Later he was to be oboe soloist with the Pocatello Symphony Orchestra, and eventually

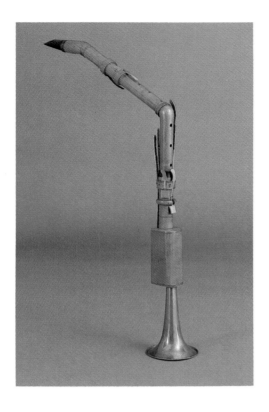

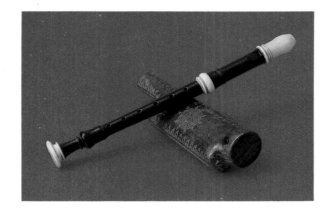

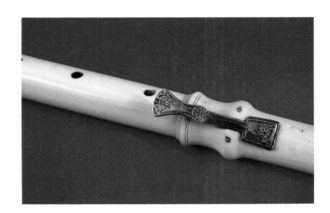

Top left: Basset-horn by Doleisch, Prague, 1793. Invented about 1770, the basset-horn was a favorite instrument of Mozart and his fellow Masons in Vienna. Board of Trustees, 1984.

Top right: Soprano recorder by Richard Haka, Amsterdam, before 1709. Arne B. and Jeanne F. Larson Endowment Fund, 1988.

Above right: Flute by Johann W. Oberlender, Nürnberg, after 1705. Ivory, one silver key. Rawlins Fund, 1986.

Below: Oboe by Klenig, Paris, ca. 1725-50. Ivory, two silver keys. Board of Trustees, 1985.

he received a scholarship to study the instrument at Brigham Young University where he earned his B.S. degree in music education in 1942. In 1951 he received his M.A. in music from San Jose State University.

During World War II, Sorensen joined the U.S. Army and was stationed at Camp Roberts, California, where he played in the 255th Army Ground Forces Band as well as in a special orchestra which played for Bing Crosby, Judy Garland, Red Skelton, and other stars.

After his release from military service, Sorensen taught for several years in Idaho; then, on September 1, 1948, he began a long career on the music faculty at San Jose State University in San Jose, California. He was also principal oboist in the Santa Clara Philharmonic Orchestra and played English horn with the San Jose Philharmonic.

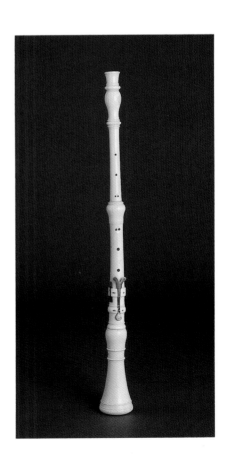

A quartet of saxophones by Adolphe Sax of Paris: a soprano in B-flat, ca. 1858; an alto in E-flat, ca. 1857; a tenor in B-flat, ca. 1861; and a baritone in E-flat, ca. 1858. The Belgian-born maker, Adolphe Sax, invented the saxophone about 1840 and was granted a fifteen-year patent in 1846, four years after having moved to Paris. Soprano, alto, and tenor, Arne B. and Jeanne F. Larson Endowment Fund, 1986. Baritone, purchase funds given by Jeannette G. Abbey, Brookings, South Dakota, 1986.

Sorensen began to collect instruments in 1948. As he notes, "They were rescued from the floors and bins of repair shops in the area. Many were purchased from Good Will, and local music stores saved instruments for me. Many productive hours were spent in the antique stores of the area, and my students, knowing of my interest, brought me many instruments."

His collecting specialty was "early Boehm-system clarinets and flutes and early key systems." Among the 145 instruments in the collection is a flute built by Cornelius Ward of London with the special key system that Ward patented in 1842; a one-keyed flute in F made by Edward Hopkins of Troy, New York, sometime after 1839; a piccolo in D-flat by George Cloos of New York, made after 1869; two matched sets of late-19th-century clarinets in A, B-flat, and C by Theo. Berteling of New York; and flutes by Boehm & Mendler, Munich, after 1867; E. Rittershausen, Berlin, after 1893; Louis Lot, Paris after 1855; and A. G. Badger, New York, before 1887. All are in splendid condition and represent some of the finest craftsmanship of the 19th century.

Also included in the collection is an 8-keyed, simple-system English flute, similar to one that Sorensen's Uncle Absalom Burris played, first in a coal miner's band in England and later in the town bands of Logan, Utah. It is a sentimental favorite.

Miniature spinet harpsichord, northern Italy, ca. 1600. Cypress, finely-pierced rose. One of the smallest, fully-working miniature harpsichords known. Ex. coll.: E.M.W. Paul. Witten-Rawlins Collection, 1984. Rests on a fortepiano by Davison & Redpath, London, 1789. This transitional instrument, built like a harpsichord but with a piano action, was once owned by Elizabeth Learned Peabody, Lake Forest, Illinois, who brought it with her, when she married, from the Learned family home in Natchez, Mississippi. Board of Trustees, 1982.

EUROPEAN KEYBOARDS

The sparkling verve of Baroque music... the varied tonal characteristics and contrasting furniture styles that marked four distinctive schools (English, Flemish, French, and Italian) of harpsichord building... early pianos for use in the home... unique cabinetry... candlelit evenings... and the romanticism of the 19th century ...all found expression — visual, as well as musical — in the keyboard instruments designed for home and concert hall.

41

Above: A tour guide shows visitors the convenient bookshelves found inside an upright grand piano by Clementi & Company, London, ca. 1815. In the foreground is a grand piano by Anton Markus Thym, Vienna, ca. 1810-15. To the right is a lyraflügel by Johann Christian Schleip, Berlin, ca. 1825, and several English square pianos, dated 1776, 1791, and 1829, designed for home use.

Left: Harpsichord by Gommarus van Everbroeck, Antwerp, 1659. The only known surviving harpsichord by one of the makers of the great 17th-century Flemish school of harpsichord building. Rawlins Fund, 1986.

"... a highly-selective collection of representative keyboard instruments."

Above: Harpsichord by Jacques Germain, Paris, 1785. The inside of the lid was repainted with romantic scenes in the 19th century, it being standard practice to repaint such instruments to reflect changing tastes in decor. French harpsichords are particularly rare. Sixty-two of them are said to have been confiscated from the Parisian nobility during the French Revolution, deposited in the Paris Conservatoire, then chopped up for firewood during the difficult winter of 1816. Rawlins Fund, 1983.

Top right: The Germain has the rich, sensuous sound for which late-18th-century French harpsichords are noted. It is heard in performance several times a year in the Museum's concert hall.

Right: Chest organ attributed to Jacob Hannss, northern Germany, ca. 1620. The hand-operated bellows supply air to 360 pipes. On-going research indicates that the organ may actually have been made in 17th-century Poland. Rawlins Fund, 1986.

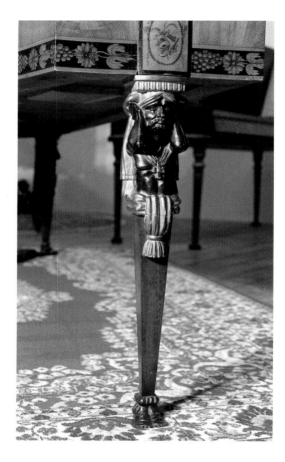

Top left: The decorated keywell of a grand piano by Anton Markus Thym, Vienna, ca. 1810-15. Rawlins Fund, 1985.

Above: Several Moors hold up the Viennese piano. Or are they covering their ears?

Left: Clavichord (detail) by Johann Paul Kraemer, Göttingen, Germany, 1804. Ex. colls.: Karl Haake, Deutsches Museum, Paul Reusch. Rawlins Fund, 1983.

Below: Harpsichord (detail) by Joseph Kirckman, London, 1798. Rawlins Fund, 1983.

Above: Fanciful brass work decorates a grand piano by William Stodart, London, ca. 1818. Board of Trustees, 1983.

Top right: Harpsichord (detail), Italy, 17th century, with later rococo decoration in the 18th-century style. Rawlins Fund, 1985.

Right: Upright grand piano (detail) by Clementi & Company, London, ca. 1815. Board of Trustees, 1981.

Below: Fortepiano (detail) by Davison & Redpath, London, 1789. Board of Trustees, 1982.

Above left: Many of the Museum's stringed instruments are shown in the Mr. and Mrs. R. E. Rawlins Gallery which one enters through iron gates designed and hand-forged by R. Walsh of Minneapolis. The gates are a gift of Constance Hampl (1906-1983) of Vermillion.

Above: Theorbo by Magnus Tieffenbrucker and bass lute by Andrea Harton, Venice, ca. 1600. Ex. coll.: Lord Astor. Witten-Rawlins Collection, 1984.

Below: Theorbo (detail) by Joachim Tielke, Hamburg, 1707. The decorative inlay is typical of Tielke, the great German maker whose instruments were much sought after by royalty and nobility. Rawlins Fund, 1986.

EUROPEAN STRINGS

Showpieces equal to those found any-where...rare, 16th-century violins, violas, and 'cellos from the north Italian cities of Brescia and Cremona, decorated for French kings and Italian nobility... superb lutes and guitars made of ivory and ebony to celebrate the splendor of Venice ...finely-detailed pochettes used by countless dancing masters...a true panoply of priceless treasures to delight the senses.

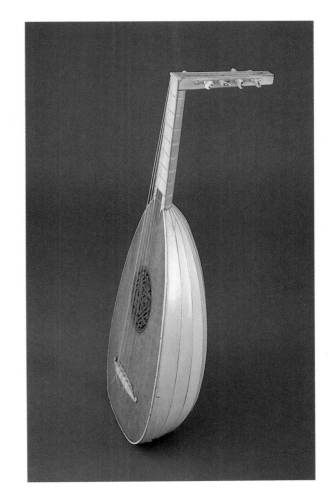

Above: Treble lute by Master D.G., Venice, ca. 1550. Dated even earlier by some experts, this is, in any case, the earliest surviving "all-ivory" lute; only the pine belly, which must be free to vibrate, is not of ivory or covered with ivory veneer. Ex. coll.: Lord Astor. Witten-Rawlins Collection, 1984.

Right: Cittern attributed to Augustinus or Franciscus citaroedus, Urbino, Italy, ca. 1550. The body, long neck, and pegbox terminating in an openwork scroll are carved from a single piece of wood. Two other citterns with the open scroll survive in London and Vienna, but do not have the elaborate body. Ex. coll.: Lord Astor. Witten-Rawlins Collection, 1984.

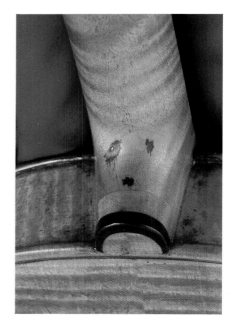

Above left: Violino piccolo by Antonio and Girolamo Amati, Cremona, 1613. Witten-Rawlins Collection, 1984. Tenor viola by Andrea Guarneri, Cremona, 1664. Witten-Rawlins Collection, 1984. The "Harrison" violin by Antonio Stradivari, Cremona, 1693. Rawlins Fund, 1985. Three great Cremonese instruments, the first two in unaltered condition.

Above: The "Harrison" is one of only a handful of Strads that survive with an original neck, lengthened slightly where it joins the body. The three nails which Stradivari used to fasten the neck to the body can still be seen. Rawlins Fund, 1985.

Left: Four magnificent violas (left to right) by Gasparo da Salò, Brescia, before 1609; Andrea Guarneri, Cremona, 1664; Peregrino di Zanetto de' Micheli, Brescia, after 1564; and Jakob Stainer, Absam, Austria, ca. 1650. Witten-Rawlins Collection, 1984.

The Witten-Rawlins Collection

Above: Violin, viola, and 'cello, three of fourteen instruments that survive by Andrea Amati, Cremona, before 1577, and a violin by his grandson Nicolo Amati, Cremona, 1628. It was in the shop of Andrea Amati that the form of the instruments of the violin family as they are known today crystallized. Witten-Rawlins Collection, 1984.

Detail: The "King," a famous 'cello by Andrea Amati, is painted and gilded with the emblems, devices, and mottoes of King Charles IX of France (d. 1574) for whom Andrea Amati made a set of instruments. Witten-Rawlins Collection, 1984.

Laurence Witten (b. 1926) began collecting in 1942. A graduate of the Yale University School of Music, he is married to Cora Williams of Atlanta, Georgia, a pianist. Since 1951 he has been an antiquarian bookseller in Southport, Connecticut, and has become well-known as a specialist in Medieval manuscripts, early printed books, and Renaissance manuscripts and books.

During the 1950s, he began to think seriously of establishing an "ideal" collection of stringed instruments. When several outstanding older collections of instruments, labels, tools, and documents — notably those of the Bisiach family in Milan and Emil Herrmann of Berlin/ New York — were broken up during the 1960s, a number of those "ideal" instruments became available.

The remarkable trio of unaltered and virtually new instruments by Cerin (1792), Gragnani (1788), and Mantegazza (1793) first came to light as a result of the Stradivari Bicentennial in 1937. The trio was united for the first time in Witten's collection.

The Andrea Guarneri tenor viola (1664) in original condition was acquired from the Bisiachs, followed by the small violin by the Brothers Amati (1613) in equally original state. Other important acquisitions were the "King Charles IX" 'cello from the Prieto collection, a Nicolo Amati violin (1628) from the Rodewald collection, already exhibited for more than a century, one of two surviving instruments by Zanetto of Brescia (before 1564), a great viola by his son Peregrino (after 1564), and a superb viola by Gasparo da Salò (before 1609).

The liquidation of the contents of Hever Castle in England by Lord

49

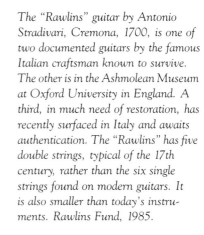

" . . . remarkable works of exquisite craftsmanship, representing some of the finest achievements of our cultural heritage."

Astor in the 1960s revealed the existence of a group of primarily Venetian plucked instruments. These, along with an ivory lute from the music room of Astor's London house, Cliveden, and a 16th-century harp from the Bisiachs, were also added to the Witten holdings.

Documentary materials in Witten's collection include important books and graphics dating back to the 16th century. Also included are the Herrmann and Bisiach collections of antique parts, fittings, tools, drawings, bridges, cases, and other items associated with the early history of violin-making, and the Salabue-Fiorini-DeWit-Herrmann collection of violinmakers' labels.

Virtually complete for important Italian makers of the 17th-19th centuries, the collection of labels was begun no later than 1804 by Count Ignazio Alessandro Cozio de Salabue, the famous Italian collector and diarist, who bought Stradivari's workshop materials from the heirs and owned many great instruments. There are more than 250 Italian labels, including five by the Amati family, eleven by the Guarneri, twenty-three by the Guadagnini, and eight by the Stradivari. In addition, there is an immense holding of non-Italian labels, especially rich in German masters, formed by the late Emil Herrmann.

The availability of the legendary Witten collection, which Museum staff had first seen and studied in 1982, became known early in December 1983. Mr. and Mrs. R. E. Rawlins, honorary members of the Museum's Board of Trustees,

The "Rawlins" guitar by Antonio Stradivari, Cremona, 1700, is one of two documented guitars by the famous Italian craftsman known to survive. The other is in the Ashmolean Museum at Oxford University in England. A third, in much need of restoration, has recently surfaced in Italy and awaits authentication. The "Rawlins" has five double strings, typical of the 17th century, rather than the six single strings found on modern guitars. It is also smaller than today's instruments. Rawlins Fund, 1985.

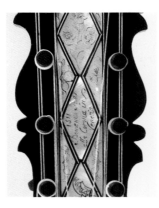

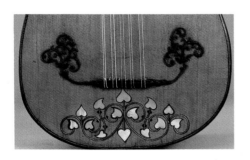

Guitar (left) by Domenico Sellas, Venice, ca. 1670. Inlaid mother-of-pearl. Arne B. and Jeanne F. Larson Endowment Fund, 1984. Guitar by Alexandre Voboam, Paris, 1670. Rawlins Fund, 1987. Members of the Sellas family in Venice and the Voboam family in Paris made many of the finest guitars of the 17th century.

offered to help purchase the collection, if the Museum could raise the rest of the needed funds. USD President Joseph M. McFadden (1982-), who later admitted that he did not think it possible to raise the money but was not about to dampen anyone's enthusiasm by saying so, gave permission to try.

However, before efforts could get underway, the Staatliches Institut für Musikforschung Preussischer Kulturbesitz in Berlin made a formal offer to purchase the collection which it planned to house in the new Musikinstrumenten-Museum next to Philharmonic Hall in Berlin. Other institutions reportedly trying to raise the funds included the Germanisches Nationalmuseum in Nürnberg, the Museum of Fine Arts in Boston, the City of Cremona, and several dealers working for unidentified collectors and museums.

The initial Berlin offer was rejected by the Witten family, but it was clear that the German negotiations would continue. Afraid that the collection would be lost, Mr. and Mrs. Rawlins called — on a Sunday night, "to save money" — and offered to purchase the collection. Negotiations were concluded at the

Witten home in Fairfield, Connecticut, on February 5, 1984.

Shortly thereafter, the Board of Trustees officially named it the Witten-Rawlins Collection. According to Barnes Abell, Chairman of the Board (1973-1986), "Larry Witten made an incredible contribution to the study of cultural history by establishing a collection of instruments and other documentary materials which systematically traces the early history of stringed-instrument making in the chief north-Italian centers of activity. At the same time, however, it was the extraordinary generosity of Bob and Marge Rawlins that made it possible to keep the collection in this country. It is only appropriate, therefore, that this marvelous resource be known hereafter as the Witten-Rawlins Collection."

Commenting on behalf of the Witten family, Laurence Witten said, "We are all very pleased that our lifelong collection is to remain in the United States, and that it has gone to an extraordinarily dynamic museum which, despite its comparatively recent formation, is rapidly developing into one of the most energetic and significant such holdings in our hemisphere."

Above left: Viola d'amore by Bernardo Calcanio, Genoa, 1742. Viola d'amore by Niccolo Gagliano, Naples, 175-. Quinton by Giovanni Grancino, Milan, 1693. Ex. coll.: Salzer. Witten-Rawlins Collection, 1984. Note the blindfolds on the violas d'amore: "love is blind."

Above: Violin, Brescian school, ca. 1640. Possibly by Antonio Mariani, Pesaro. The original neck and pegbox terminates in a finely-carved lioness (the symbol of Brescia). Violin by Gio. Paolo Maggini, Brescia, before 1632. Witten-Rawlins Collection, 1984.

Below: Violin bow, ca. 1680. The hair passes through the mouth of a finely-carved ebony lion. Witten-Rawlins Collection, 1984.

Above (left to right): Four little dancing master's fiddles. Pochette, Bohemia, ca. 1600-50. Board of Trustees, 1979. Kit attributed to Richard Tobin, London, early 19th century. Board of Trustees, 1980. Pochette bow by John Dodd, London, late 18th century. Board of Trustees, 1980. Pochette, France, mid-17th century; ivory body with tortoiseshell fingerboard. Rawlins Fund, 1985. Pochette, France, mid-17th century. Witten-Rawlins Collection, 1984.

Right: Hardingfele by Olav Lomundal, Hoston Orkdal, Norway, 1966. The Norwegian national folk instrument. Four melody and four sympathetic strings. Arne B. Larson Collection, 1979.

Below: Nyckelharpa (keyed fiddle), Sweden, 19th century. The Swedish national folk instrument. This example was brought to the United States and still played by Knut Stone of Salem, South Dakota, in the mid-20th century. Arne B. Larson Collection, 1979.

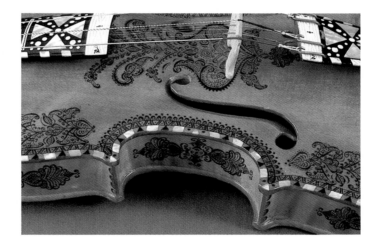

AMERICAN INSTRUMENTS

A nostalgic tribute to America's musical history and to the settlers who brought their love of music to her vast territories... the brass instruments of the Civil War... the years when town bands were a dominant factor in American cultural life... turn-of-the-century mandolins, guitars, and banjos... barrel 'cellos, stove-pipe 'cellos, and cigar-box fiddles ... all of it pure Americana.

Top: One of the features of the Mr. and Mrs. Clifford E. Graese Gallery is this exhibit of instruments used during the American Civil War, including drums and over-the-shoulder horns for the infantry and circular helicons for the cavalry.

Above: Snare drum by Eli Brown, Windsor, Connecticut, ca. 1825. Arne B. Larson Collection, 1979. Snare drum by H.R. Eisenbrandt, Baltimore, after 1860. Board of Trustees, 1981. Over-the-shoulder cornet in B-flat by Klemm & Bro., Philadelphia, ca. 1862. Board of Trustees, 1981. Cornet in E-flat by John F. Stratton, New York, after 1860. Arne B. Larson Collection, 1979.

Above: The Norris Harp Orchestra (harp, violin, and drums) played for dances in South Dakota, 1906-08. Harp by Sebastian Erard, London, 1812. Given to USD by Mrs. J.W. Norris, Yankton, South Dakota, 1935. Violin by Johann Glass, Leipzig, 1904. Gift of Mrs. Ralph Burrell, Elk Point, South Dakota, 1980.

Top right: Phonograph by Thomas A. Edison, Orange, New Jersey, ca. 1910. Arne B. Larson Collection, 1979.

Right: Stan Fritts (1910-69) led the Korn Kobblers, a nationally-known dance and novelty band, from 1938 to 1954. Washboard with electric auto horns, siren, klaxon, doorbell, whistle, woodblock, and twenty-one auto and bicycle horns. Gift of Blanche Fritts, Yankton, South Dakota, 1986.

55

Above left: Upright piano by Decker Brothers, New York, ca. 1891. Unique keyboard invented by Paul von Janko, a Hungarian musician and engineer, in 1882. Gift of Mrs. Merritt A. Williamson, Nashville, Tennessee, 1987, in memory of her husband. Grand harmonicon by Francis Hopkinson Smith, Baltimore, ca. 1825. Twenty-four glasses. Gift of Mrs. Fred Glover, Jr., Charlotte, North Carolina, 1987. Grand piano by Chickering, Boston, ca. 1884. Gift of Ravenswood Congregational Church, Chicago/Yankton College, 1970.

Above: Upright grand piano (detail) by Schimmel & Nelson, Fairbault, Minnesota, ca. 1889. Arne B. Larson Collection, 1979.

Left: American reed organ by Mason & Risch, Worcester, Massachusetts, ca. 1895. Vocalion model. The pipes are an ornamental facade. Arne B. Larson Collection, 1979.

Above: Square grand piano by Wm. Knabe & Co., Baltimore, 1891. Gift of Max Siler Wehrly, Arlington, Virginia, 1980, in memory of his mother, Maude Siler Wehrly (1877-1955).

Above right: Pianoforte by John Kearsing from London for J.J. Rickers, New York, ca. 1825. Gold trim. Gift of Marilynn L. Collins, Flossmoor, Illinois, 1981, in memory of her father, Wyman H. Carey, pianist.

Right: Three American reed organs in the E. Mildred Lewison Gallery, the first by W. W. Kimball, Chicago, ca. 1876, the other two by Story & Clark, Chicago, late 19th century. Arne B. Larson Collection, 1979.

The Golden Age of Bands

Each year faculty and advanced students from the University of South Dakota's Department of Music use the Museum's resources to form *The Golden Age of Bands 1865-1915*, a unique ensemble that re-creates that great 50-year period of our musical heritage known as the "Golden Age of Bands" in America. First organized by Arne B. Larson in 1967, it is the only active collegiate ensemble in the country devoted to the authentic performance of the instrumental music enjoyed by Americans during the years between the Civil War and World War I.

Original music and period instruments are used, including Albert-system clarinets and conical-bore brasses. The pitch is nearly half a step above the A-440 used today, and the scoring of the music is different, as well, with tenor horns instead of trombones, no saxophones, and E-flat cornets and clarinets adding extra brilliance to the sound. The result is rousing band music with a unique timbre and variety of sound that is once again new and exciting.

Top: The Golden Age of Bands 1865-1915 featured a wide variety of brass instruments.

Above: A cornet in E-flat by C.G. Conn, Elkhart, Indiana, 1882, and a cornet in B-flat by Antoine Courtois, Paris, ca. 1890, are played during USD's annual re-creation of a turn-of-the-century concert in the park. Arne B. Larson Collection, 1979.

Left: Cornet in B-flat by Frank Holton & Co., Chicago, ca. 1910. Gold-plated. Gift of Mrs. G. R. Miller, Canton, South Dakota, 1974, in memory of her husband.

Above: "Raincatcher" Sousaphone in E-flat by H. N. White Co., Cleveland, Ohio, ca. 1910. The first Sousaphones—of which the Museum has eight examples—had bells that pointed straight up; hence their nickname, the "raincatcher."
Arne B. Larson Collection, 1979.

Top right: USD's unique ensemble, The Golden Age of Bands 1865-1915, performs annually, including concerts for the American Bandmasters Association, the American Musicological Society, and the American Musical Instrument Society.

Right: Soprano slide saxophone by Reiffel & Husted, Chicago, ca. 1920. The only example known to survive.
Arne B. Larson Collection, 1979.

Below: A selection of harmonicas from the Museum's collections. Gift of Clay H. Johnson, Jr., O'Neill, Nebraska, 1978-79.

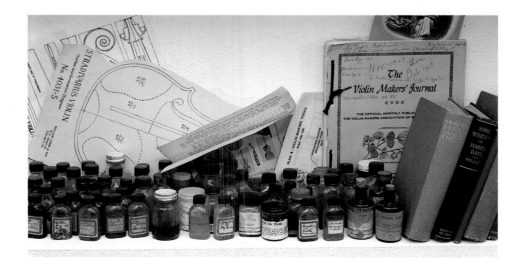

Top: The Stanley G. Newton Violin Workshop. Gift of Marie Newton, Ottumwa, Iowa, 1972-73. Stanley G. Newton (1911-1971), like his father, studied, repaired, and made violins in Ottumwa, Iowa.

Left: Violin by Emil Widhalm, Nürnberg, late 19th century. Sold by J. W. Pepper, Philadelphia. Gift of Clay Johnson, Jr., O'Neill, Nebraska, 1981.

Below: Violin repair requires a wide variety of varnishes.

". . . a tribute to the immigrants who brought their music to America."

Above: Pure Americana! Palmer N. Roe (1888-1966) of Canton, South Dakota, served in France in World War I, was a deputy county sheriff, and made and played several unusual instruments, now preserved at the Museum.

Top right: Barrel 'cello by Palmer Roe, Canton, South Dakota, ca. 1955. Arne B. Larson Collection, 1979.

Far right: Banjo by George Washburn, Chicago, early 20th century. Cigar box fiddle by Walter Pelke, Minneapolis, 1935. Built as a W.P.A. project. Arne B. Larson Collection, 1979.

Below right: Symphony harp guitar by W.J. Dyer & Bro., St. Paul, Minnesota, early 20th century. Gift of Arne B. Larson, 1981.

Preserving a Priceless Legacy

Hidden from public view, but at the heart of The Shrine to Music Museum, the conservation laboratory is a fascinating place where consummate craftsmanship and the latest in technological knowledge come together in a careful blend. The world's cultural heritage is a precious resource — irreplaceable when lost, rarely regained when seriously impaired. Thus, to protect and conserve important cultural artifacts is to preserve a priceless legacy for all people today and in future generations. The study of human culture through material artifacts has become a distinct discipline in which the skill and the insight of the conservator and the instrumentation of the scientist are indispensable.

Conservation is the Museum's top priority. Musical instruments are essentially fragile. The ravages of time and neglect can affect not only the basic stability of the instruments but also effectively destroy their ability to act, in the way originally intended, as sound-producing mediums.

At first impression, the job of the Museum's conservator might seem overwhelming, with more than 4,500 instruments to preserve — many of them hundreds of years old and few in perfect condition. How does one man meet the challenge?

"The first rule of the conservator is not to do any more than is necessary at the moment," explains the Museum's conservator, Gary Stewart. "Some wear and tear marks are unique to the instrument, and we are under an obligation to preserve a document that will speak from

Left: The Museum's collections are used for research projects by graduate students and scholars from this country and abroad. The E-flat tubas were cataloged in 1983 by John Swain, Professor of Music at California State University, Los Angeles, for his Ph. D. from Michigan State University.

Right: An integral part of the care of the instruments in the conservation laboratory is the photographic documentation of each phase of the treatment.

Above: Brice Dupin de Saint Cyr, a Parisian violin maker, spent a week at the Museum in 1985. He is one of a growing number of English, French, Italian, and German visitors who have been attracted to the Museum by the Witten-Rawlins Collection.

Right: Gary M. Stewart, conservator, prepares the "Janko piano" (see p. 56) for exhibition in the Lewison Gallery.

the past. It is definitely worse to do too much—than to do nothing—which sometimes makes the job a bit easier."

The conservator determines the extent of the conservation and/or restoration of each instrument in consultation with the director. Original-type materials are used whenever possible. Procedures must be reversible. No more is done than is necessary to preserve the artifact for its intended function. And complete written and photographic documentation is prepared and maintained for future reference.

In addition, stable temperature and humidity levels must be maintained in the Museum's galleries and study-storage areas. The Museum recently completed a major renovation project designed to upgrade its climate-control system to provide optimum environmental conditions for its collections.

The galleries are under constant surveillance to prevent theft or vandalism. Permissible light levels have been determined and are maintained. The objects are carefully mounted, and display materials are tested to be certain that they will not contaminate the objects. The conservator makes routine surveys of the instruments in the galleries, as well as in the study-storage areas, to be certain that they remain structurally stable; and, although air pollution is negligible, the conservator cleans those items which occasionally require such attention.

The Shrine to Music Museum is a recognized model for the care and conservation of musical instruments.

63

Visiting The Shrine to Music Museum

The Shrine to Music Museum is located at the corner of Clark and Yale streets on the south edge of the University of South Dakota campus in Vermillion. Built on a bluff overlooking the Missouri River in the southeastern corner of the state, Vermillion is on South Dakota Highway 50, six miles west of the interchange with Interstate 29 (linking Kansas City, Omaha, Sioux City, Sioux Falls, Fargo, and Winnipeg). Interstate 29 can be reached from either of two major east-west interstates: I-80 (New York to San Francisco) or I-90 (Boston to Seattle).

For those planning to arrive by air, Vermillion is best served by the Sioux Falls, South Dakota, and the Sioux City, Iowa, airports. "Gateway" cities to the area are Minneapolis/St. Paul, Chicago, St. Louis, and Denver. Major carriers serving the area include America West, Continental, Delta, Northwest Orient, TWA, and United. Cars may be rented at either airport, both of which are served by the major rental agencies.

Motels, restaurants, parks, and picnic areas are all to be found within walking distance of the Museum. Ample camping facilities are available in the area, and there are unlimited recreational opportunities at nearby Lewis & Clark Lake.

Free parking for Museum visitors is available in a lot on the east side of the building. When the lot is full, street parking is always available two or three blocks south on Yale Street. Handicapped parking is in the northwest corner of the lot. A wheelchair entrance with an elevator is on the north side of the building; ring the doorbell and wait for admittance. Restrooms, including handicapped facilities, are on the main floor.

An introductory sound/slide show, which describes the history and development of the Museum, its collections, and its programs, can be viewed in the Arne B. Larson Concert Hall. It is highly recommended for first-time visitors.

Catalogs of the Museum's collections, color post-cards, copies of this book, and recordings of music performed on original, period instruments may be purchased at the information desk in the main lobby.

There are many photographic opportunities at the Museum and cameras may be used without permission. However, permission is required for use of tripods or other equipment. Requests for permission to reproduce photographs of exhibits and instruments must be made in writing.

There is no admission charge. However, contributions are encouraged. Membership information is available at the information desk. Guidelines for access to the collections for research purposes are also available at the desk.

The Museum is open daily, except Thanksgiving, Christmas, and New Year's, Monday-Friday, 9:00 to 4:30, Saturday, 10:00 to 4:30, and Sunday, 2:00 to 4:30. Group tours are available upon request. Call (605) 677-5306 for further information.

Private gifts are essential for the continued growth and development of The Shrine to Music Museum. The Museum is pleased to apply gift funds in the manner specified by the donor and to recognize major supporters in terms mutually agreeable. All gifts are tax deductible within the limits provided by law.

Donations do not have to be made in the form of cash. Spring cleaning could produce some "white elephants" that might be of real value if donated as a tax-deductible contribution. Gifts of real property, art objects, and antiques have been received in recent years. Vehicles, homes, and farms have also been donated. Anyone interested in making a gift of this kind should contact the Director of the Museum at (605) 677-5306. All inquiries are kept strictly confidential.